This book belongs to...

_____

Illustrated by Mary Lonsdale

Published in Great Britain by Brimax,
An imprint of Autumn Publishing Group
Appledram Barns, Chichester, PO20 7EQ

Published in the US by Byeway Books Inc,
Lenexa KS 66219 Tel 866.4BYEWAY
www.byewaybooks.com

Words and Pictures

First Words

BRIMAX

The classroom

table

chair

book

 **paintbrush**

blackboard

crayon

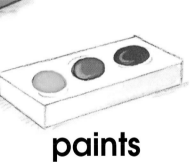

pencil

paints

picture

What is on the blackboard?

The supermarket

bag

cheese

orange

money

bread

eggs

carrot

bottle

tomato

How many tomatoes are in the bag?

The birthday party

cookies

candles

 **cake**

 **party hat**

 **drink**

 **balloon**

 **present**

 **card**

 **plate**

Point to the child who is blowing out the candles.

The farm

barn

tractor

 **hen**

 **horse**

farmer

pig

cow

dog

sheep

Can you find the cat?

The park

skateboard

bat

kite

swing

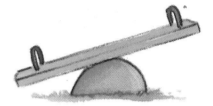

see-saw

boat

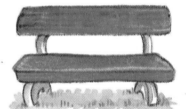

bench

slide

bike

Can you find the duck?

The kitchen

spoon  cupboard  knife

toaster

stove

cup

plate

bowl

sink

What do you have for your breakfast?

Playtime

plane

truck

ball  **train**  **doll**

storybook

teddy bear

car

telephone

Can you find the frog?

Bedtime

bed

quilt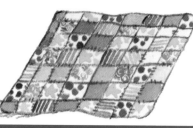

stars

lamp

teddy bear

slippers

mirror

pillow

moon

Can you find the toy rabbit?

Here are some of the words in this book.
Can you read them and find the matching picture?

card

dog

cookies

bread

table

cheese

farmer

barn

present

picture

train

truck

bike

pillow

bowl

telephone

kite

swing

bed

toaster

Can you remember the new words you have learned?

1. What are the children sitting on?

2. What are they drawing with?

★

3. What do you put shopping in?

4. What vegetables can you see?

★

5. What do you take to a party?

6. What are on top of the cake?

Answers:

1. Chairs. 2. Pencils and crayons. 3. A bag. 4. Carrots and cauliflowers. 5. A present and card. 6. Candles. 7. The pig. 8. The tractor. 9. A bike. 10. A kite. 11. A bowl. 12. A stove. 13. A mirror. 14. A bed.

7. Which animal is being fed?

8. What is the hen sitting on?

 ★

9. What is in front of the tree?

10. What is the girl flying?

 ★

11. What do you put cereal in?

12. What do you cook food on?

 ★

13. What can you see yourself in?

14. What do you sleep in at night?

Guidance notes

★ This series is designed to encourage children to enjoy learning and to become successful readers at home and at school.

★ Learning is aided by repetition; the words in this book will help children to learn as they look back and repeat the words and answer the questions.

★ Stress and worry can affect a child's ability to learn so remember to make reading time fun. Children who struggle to learn at school have proven to benefit from reading sessions with adults at home, in a familiar and supportive environment.

★ As children become more confident, they should be encouraged to read the words for themselves. If a child gets a word wrong, simply correct the word and then move on to another.